AT SOME APPOINTED TIME

poems by

Catherine Harnett

Finishing Line Press
Georgetown, Kentucky

AT SOME APPOINTED TIME

for Barbara

ACKNOWLEDGMENTS

This Summer's Boys, *Dialogist*
Grim Reaper, Live at Eleven, *Dance Macabre*
Execution, *Innisfree*
Given, *Poetry Quarterly*
Garden of the Dispossessed Favorites, *Honeypot*
This Place, Once Paradise accepted by *The Transnational*
Mutt, Solstice, Conundrum written for *Tupelo Press 30/30*
Until, Northern *Virginia Review*
Obit, *Gargoyle*
Battlefield Weather, *Haunted Waters*

Publisher: Leah Maines
Editor: Christen Kincaid
Cover Art: Angelica Shaw
Author Photo: Angelica Shaw
Cover Design: Elizabeth Maines McCleavy

Printed in the USA on acid-free paper.
Order online: www.finishinglinepress.com
also available on amazon.com

Author inquiries and mail orders:
Finishing Line Press
P. O. Box 1626
Georgetown, Kentucky 40324
U. S. A.

Table of Contents

WISH

We tell our children, as they're
lulled to sleep, that stars

are made for wishing on, the
man in the moon winks at us

each night. In truth, we are
blind to what goes on above;

black holes commit stellar
homicide, the moon turns red

as blood, earth is passing through
a riot of cosmic dust.

The light that reaches us was
born before Da Vinci, Galileo,

the brightness of baby stars will
be seen millennia from now.

When we look up, it is the past
we see; too hard to comprehend.

We fib to our nestled little ones,
tell them planets know their names,

read them Goodnight Moon, recite old
nursery rhymes we learned when we

were young, when we wished on stars
as old as God.

VENIAL, MORTAL

They take up little room, venial
sins, small black dots on the soul,
leaving space for more.

Not like the big ones, mortal: they fill
the soul with blackness, leave no room
for sanctifying grace.

Lust, Gluttony, Greed, Sloth, Wrath,
Envy, Pride, seven and deadly; unless
confessed, there is no hope for Heaven.

Venial ones are not so clear, such a
fine line between *slightly bad* and
 pretty bad: very bad, on the precipice.

So begins a life of splitting hairs: is it a sin
to keep the extra change, to park illegally,
to love someone you should not?

How many Masses can be skipped before
God disapproves? Gossip, laziness, the Lord's
name taken in vain: what is the tipping point?

The heart wants what it wants, it keeps the soul
on edge, ready to be stained. Which of the deadly
sins will the heart commit?

We crave one more drink, the must-have
coat, fancy cars; the too-young girl behind
the counter, delicate and lithe; what we lust
for, mortal and dark.

CONUNDRUM

Luck is in a box left at your door.
Used to be you needed to sign for it, or
pay the C.O.D. Now it's come what may.

A passer-by might think no one will know
what I did, light-fingered and sly. Does it
become a box of bad luck then? After all,
several sins have been committed; there
surely must be retribution.

A neighbor takes the box for safekeeping.
After some time, he becomes curious, begins
to hope you won't come home; it's his isn't it?
possession being nine tenths of the law?
What sort of luck does he own then?

When you come home, there's an odd box
on the porch, no return address. Authorities
warn against opening mail you do not recognize.
These days a shrapnel bomb, anthrax, the finger
of a stranger wrapped in tissue can signal you
are in someone's sights.

The box must be destroyed to learn if it
is safe or not. Is it good luck to find it held
nothing to cause you harm? Or bad? You
have no idea what its contents were; maybe
a jewel, a bundle of fifties, the grand prize.

Luck is delivered to your door. It might be
stolen, tempting, something to be wary of.
What kind is in the box? Lady Luck, a stroke
of luck; good luck, pure dumb luck or that
smug little yellow thing, a lucky duck?

COMING TO GRIEF

ONE.   CHARLESTON, DARK

The June night's heat, the insomniac beast
prowls. Call it instinct, rage, imperative;
you cannot change a tiger's need to feast.
For him, there is no other way to live.

His hunger calls him to a sacred place
built for praise, contrition, forgiveness, prayer.
Sinners and saints in this house of hope, grace
in which God dwells. This holy place stands where

it once burned, red flames fed by hate-stoked crime.
Why does God stand by and let evil win,
let the good, the young die before their time?
The beast decrees it is their time, their skin

condemning them, the dark color of night.
Picks them off, one by one in God's clear sight.

TWO.   ANNIVERSARY

Brandon loved Angry Birds, Shana slept with Fetch, her Labrador. Alana was
Mulan for Halloween and the moon fascinated Scott. Renee, Jason, autistic
Austin, Charlotte, Alex; and more first graders making lists for Santa,
loud and wriggling in their seats.

At ten to noon, the boy walked in, unannounced, picked them off one
by one. A pair of girls hid under desks, Mark wet his pants, others clung
to Mrs. Johnson's denim skirt. They all went, too.

This time of year always calls them back; their names are read in the town
square, a moment of silence at eleven-fifty.

This is the place children always came to carol, dress as Magi or sheep, where the
Mayor donned his Santa suit, little ones so proud of being good all
year. The done-up Christmas tree, the manger scene with lambs and hay, plump
baby Jesus. Could He see the coming tragedies, His, theirs?

THREE. HOW MANY MORE

By now, everyone knows something: where
the boy was that night, how his hands were
tied; no word on who's responsible. No one's
talking. No one ever does.

"May he rest in peace," Pastor prays, blessing
the boy's soul on its way Heavenward.

At the graveside, powdered ladies with their
paper fans, Amens; a sea of Sunday hats moves
towards the hall. Miss Alma's flowers dazzle;
so does the ham prepared by Pastor's niece, her
special recipe other churchwomen covet.

What more is there to say? The boy's mother,
wild with grief, has taken to her bed. The hall
empties out, baskets of biscuits, pitchers of sweet
tea, left on the sad tables. Pastor bids farewell
to ladies in their wilted hats, wishes them safe home.

Like Pastor, Deaconess is wrought; she knows
there will be more; earth preparing to receive
young men, boys really, simply walking home
in the early dark, suspected. How can she
glorify God, proclaim his mercy, knowing this?

But she is God's servant, calls on Him for grace:
to forget, to love, not loathe the sight of white sheets
billowing on her neighbor's laundry line.
Let them be angel wings, cumulous, dove.

FOUR. THE DAY AFTER THE DAY AFTER

It is all well and good, the day
after. So many embraces, promises,
open hearts. Bouquets and teddy bears,
candles and messages; and the hordes
of mourners, a well of tears. Forgiveness
reigns, and mercy; such gorgeous
tributes to the gone!

What happens on the day after the day
after? Wilted flower must be collected,
stuffed animals carted off to the children's
ward, thousands of messages catalogued.
Good intentions abound.

The days after the days become months
and years; there is a reservoir of ready
tears; hearts will swell at a future time,
and a time after that; another surfeit of
roses will line the streets and church
entryways, an echo of the time before,
and the time before that.

THIS SUMMER'S BOYS
(after Columbine)

In the bright blue of this town pool, they dive
and howl, their sharp shoulder blades are clipped
angel wings, their drenched neon trunks, their rail-thin
bones. Here at summer's height, they seek the deeper
end where nothing matters but the gasps their dives
attract, one's graceful arc, the other's clumsy flop.

For now they are content to clown and tumble,
these days of sunlight, brown parched grass.
Who knows if someday, one of them is shunned,
strange music sung in his dark room; who knows
if one of them will take the long bright gun or blade,
hold it close to his once-summer skin, and hunt that
boy who dove with him, surprise his skinny soul.

HARAM

Girls learn how to read, how
to add, subtract. They giggle,
sitting on the dirt floor of this
make-do school.

Men arrive in the middle of
the day to carry out decrees;
only they have permission
to open books.

So many girls dying to learn.
Their young bones and open
minds. They pay for loving
words so much, and numbers,
and the way a clean blouse feels
against their skin.

COLLISION

Even in Antigny, life intrudes. Two trapped women in their Opel,
overturned, returning from the funeral of a friend.

You stop to help, wait for the gendarmes to come and take details.
How like you, to speak gently to the driver buckled in, her blue hair

stained with blood; her sister, impossible to rouse.

Doesn't it all come down to being somewhere at an appointed time,
without a hint of what's to come?

There isn't time to pack a bag. We just show up, que sera.

Tell that to the shoppers in the marketplace at noon, who mingle
with the man who pulls the pin and takes them down with him.

Or the mother and her child in the parking lot who meet a wild
boy desperate for a car.

Or the driver, late for work one January day, waiting for the light
to change as the foreign gunman fires.

Or the child snatched in broad daylight, or the father on the downed
plane. And on and on and on.

After the ambulance leaves, in the darkening light of Burgundy,
you write to tell me of your day.

Here, on another continent, I write about my quiet days, listening
for my baby's breath two doors down.

I tend to impatiens and petunias. I have no hint what lies ahead;
whether I will stall on the railroad track, the thoroughfare,

walk on the city street where anything can happen, any time to me,
to him, to them at some appointed time and place.

What will be will be will be.

OBIT

I remember when I was beautiful, you, cocky,
irresistible. We could not get enough: Singapore,
Bangkok, the mountain cabin; and that bar
in Arlington which smelled like beer, where we met
even on the day snow paralyzed the town.

I drove past there on Saturday. The bar now caters
to another clientele. And the Queen Bee where
we ordered Hanoi pork and Singha. And the pool
hall, pawnshop, everything is gone.

I read the Post each morning, scan the page to find
your name, rehearse the pang I'll feel when
it comes true. I cannot grasp that someday you
will leave this earth. Someone I completely loved,
buried in your parents' plot. Gone: your warm hands,
the shoulder where the bullet lodged; to think
the earth will claim the body I embraced, on loan
to me for eleven years.

Obituaries do not tell the truth. Yes, you are the son
of, brother of, father of. They have it right, which high
school you attended, where you worked. Obituaries do
not tell the truth entirely. Yours will leave me out, I
will not be included in the list of loved ones surviving
you. I will be your hidden widow, even though we
were not joined by law, invisible, unnamed, surviving you.

Each day ticks; I will read that you have passed.
You will not wake from sleep as you once did;
I watched your lungs, your heart rise, fall, inside
their cave, in love with the sound of them, even
knowing that you had to leave; but not like this.

HENRY, SUMMER

This is not about the whip marks
on his back or the brand on his
shoulder or that he never saw his
children after June two years ago.
It is not about a man tied with a
rope to the spreading elm, for what
Margaret James said he did. It is
about Henry and my mother and
me sitting on the front steps with
clean wash, and fanning ourselves
like ladies in their Sunday hats do
at church. This is about the way
Henry talks like one of us reading
Genesis and speaking good English
which he learned in Charleston
where his wife was bought and his
children sold to another family.
And the way my mother and him
converse, and her cheeks red, not
from the outside temperature.
How he laughs when she tries to
pair the wrong socks up and how
polite he is when my mother offers
lemonade, thank you ma'am. I
imagine it's just me and him on
the porch talking and he looks right
through me with his brown dark
eyes and all I have to do is tell
on him and he becomes another
roped man on a tree. And did
Margaret James feel like I do now,
warm in places I don't know the
names of, and does my mother
feel like that, sitting close to him,
when he looks deep at her, and
what will happen if my father knows.

BATTLEFIELD WEATHER

Boxwood, magnolia, pink crepe myrtle; not birch, scrub pine, lilac. Southern trees, the sharp smell of hedges in hot June, summer's white harsh light. I am from fish-shaped Paumanok, Whitman called it, Long Island, where I sought out crocus in the hard March ground, and read under the summer sycamore.

When I came south, I did not know I would be here so long, driving into D.C. for over thirty years, on 95 and 50, 236 and 66, miles of headlights and tail lights. The city comes to work early, leaves late, this place of politics and law, the rich and very poor. In summertime, the men are in seersucker, bow ties, shirts rumpled by four o'clock. Mosquitoes, miasma, the lassitude of southern ladies with their done-up hair. These people work next to me; I am as foreign to them as they are to me. I will never be a debutante, never drink sweet tea, eat collard greens.

*

I have had eight addresses, some under my married name; those years we picked apples near Winchester, drove to farm stands, which have since disappeared, honeymooned at Wintergreen.

Virginia enveloped us, each season tasted different, smelled distinct.

*

I buried my parents in Leesburg city, the Courthouse in its center, lawyers rushing to file motions. I am their executor, meeting in the quiet offices in historic houses which have seen better days. I sit and hear the large clock tick and notice the slanting wooden floor. Things go so slowly here, four years to finalize my parents' small estate.

Married or alone, I've made a garden each spring, planting flowers in dense clay; some take, persisting through months, some humid, some dry as bone. And through winters, unpredictable, harsh enough to close everything.

*

In summer, storms come in late afternoon: lightning, gusts, the crack of thunder, hot rain. The air does not cool afterwards. There is the smell of sulphur, you can see steam rise from asphalt. Frightful, *thunderous*, lethal. We see the sickly yellow sky, and hide in basements till it is safe.

*

In such a thunderstorm, September 1862, the Battle of Ox Hill.
Gunpowder was useless in the rain. Soldiers turned to bayonets, fighting
hand-to-hand, lunging at the enemy. Historians described it as a minor,
inconclusive battle. Two Union Generals lost, 2100 Confederates and Union
troops dead. With such losses, it is beyond me to call this minor.
I live a mile from there, Ox Hill, Chantilly. In memory, there is a
battlefield park tucked between houses, a quiet enclave, and wide,
with grass the color of wheat.

To think that so much blood was spilt in a close-by field, by so
many inconsequential soldiers, from North and South.

*

> I live among the ghosts
> of felled boys carrying
> tintypes of sweethearts,
> boys who never took
> to the marriage bed, sired
> sons, felt a wife's hand
> on their skin
>
> I feel them underfoot,
> under concrete as I shop,
> a small plaque where
>
> General Lee arrived,
> a preserved cornfield
> where boys spilled blood,
> fighting to keep other boys
> in chains

*

I see the Blue Ridge Mountains from the overpass. Their full gentle outline
contrasts against the slipshod stores and eateries on Lee-Jackson Highway, the
war route east towards Washington.

There is so much more: stunning mountains, Shenandoah, Appalachian, and
rivers, Potomac, and the New River, the oldest on the continent, flowing south to
north; Luray's ancient crystal caves, Skyline Drive, words do no justice.

From the overpass, Blue Ridge looks sheltering and deep, and sometimes I catch
my breath.

*

My father teaches me about the war. We have come to Gettysburg to see the diorama, little soldiers and their maneuvers. I am twelve and mostly bored, first regiments and companies and generals' names mean nothing. But then, the photographs of Gettysburg, 1863, the insufferable heat of July.

We stop at Devil's Den, photographs of dead Confederates, the litter of war: rifles, canteens, shredded uniforms, *slaughter pen* as it was called, men trapped between boulders in smoldering July. I never forgot; all the young men, bleeding blue and grey and red.

My father read *Andersonville*, about the prison where 14,000 Union soldiers died; Walt Whitman saw men who survived the camp and was horrified. "There are deeds, crimes that may be forgiven, but this is not among them," he wrote.

*

The book was so disturbing, my mother hid it in the dresser drawer.

*

At fourteen I am a Confederate sympathizer, having a secret love affair with Ashley Wilkes, not Rhett like the other girls. Genteel, honorable, an officer, not a privateer who frequents brothels. My friends make fun of me for choosing the wimp. I am realistic, I would never stand a chance, no selfless, saccharine Melanie, or Scarlett, the tease. From New York, too rough around the edges.

I am in love, too, with Scout and Frankie and Eugene, southern children who live in the books I read. The atmosphere of heat and longing and loss touch and haunt me, the secrets and eccentricity pull me in, even to this day.

*

> Cheat Mountain, Days Gap,
> Deep Bottom, Yellow Tavern,
> simple names, simple towns
> where war barged in; I love
> the names of these places,
> Hatchers Run, Mortons Ford,
> Swift Creek.

*

I am driving 95 South, past Richmond, ninety miles from home, Virginia's capital, once the Confederacy's. A demarcation line between victory and vanquished, where the real South starts.

Faulkner said "garrulous outraged baffled ghosts" have haunted the South since its defeat. I am sure that I've seen some, and I am still afraid of them.

Intolerance, Bibles, the poor in mountain shacks, guns, the ignorant.
The Southern Cross, defiance: the young man in his pickup, a flapping flag, cranked-up Country loudening the air.

*

My father drives me to Williamsburg and Yorktown, where another war was fought; towards Jamestown, old settlement, so many lost to the Seasoning. This is Virginia, too, where American liberty was born. Blood shed to unify, not divide.

*

After Richmond, it comes home to me: I have lived here so long I cannot deny that *this is home. Where I have lived for over thirty years, My northern heart has made a truce.*

*

My daughter attends a Southern school with in-state benefits, because we reside, we have put down roots here, to my surprise, we are *Virginians.*

*

I will live in an emptied nest till she graduates; years of rabid heat, perplexing snow. Violent battlefield weather.

*

I will give Virginia its due, driving alone to places I have never seen: Dismal Swamp, Roanoke, Chincoteague, to see ponies swim; to Shenandoah, Cumberland and Amelia counties; Lake Louisa.

In spring, planting hosta and verbena, I will experience again the wiles of clay, and how things grow at this latitude, near the cornfield where so many left their bodies to ascend.

THRALL

You could say I caused her harm; she was meant
to be harmed. You could say I took her youth away;
it was there for the taking.

I possessed the wet pink parts, showered her with gifts,
the whalebone corset, nice and tight around her ribs, the
silk handkerchief to bind her hands. Of course she craved it,
hot candlewax along her spine, the occasional strap, the
way I yanked the tangle of sienna curls.

I insisted she keep an unlocked door, await my arrival,
lunch alone, wear modest clothes in greys and browns.
Captivity, she called it, overwrought as I dressed one
night to leave.

I reined her in, bought small gifts, earrings, Emeraude,
a satin blouse to cover my work, raised and red, the price
she paid for loving me. We shared the meat of animals,
dined well. But her demands, tears: we could hardly
eat out without a scene.

She gave an ultimatum: choose her, or let her go.
Such an easy choice.

I went on to have others; it was thrilling to seduce,
be seduced; years of fine wine and badinage. Some
of them I remember, most not, sometimes just an
odd detail-- a birthmark the color of café au lait.

But none of them compares to her, my caged bird.

I am mad, imagining who owns her now. A banker
with assets? An office clerk, doctor? A rough laborer?
Is it wrong to wish that she appeal to no one, past her
expiration date, her hair thin in places I feasted?

What does she say when a lover asks about the scars,
minor as they are. An accident, a father's punishment?
Or the truth: they are love's souvenirs.

The burn on her left hip, a masterpiece. Uneven
like a melanoma, pink in the center, my brand.

EDGE

A night when only the
thinnest edge of moon
was visible. She stood at
her vanity, brushing her
black hair, having changed
her mind about the promise
to give each of them a chance,
those boys from town.

You know what it's like to have
your heart set on getting what
it wants; and when things change,
there is no going back. It wants
what's owed.

One boy shrugged it off, the
other could not let it go, and
ran his knife across her neck;
tit for tat.

We watch our true crime show
as we always do on Saturday,
so many variations on a theme.
I am bothered by that girl and
the rejected boy, their photographs
spread across the screen, both
looking average, happy.

A spring moon rebuffs the chill
tonight, and as we nestle close, I
realize that I am in your hands:
my life is yours for the taking.

EXECUTION

His last wish is plum or peach,
fruit with something pink around the pit,
there is so much fruit. So much juice
that lingers on the chin, one sweet bite
to break the skin. He has never wanted
anything so much, except that girl who sent
him here, her stunned glance when he finished
up. There is nothing left except the hours.

We lie together on our bed and watch the news
unfold. There is no clemency. After years, our hands
no longer touch. Nothing lingers on the skin. Pears
languish on our tree, once bountiful, filling bowls
throughout our house. There is nothing left for us
except the hours and hours. There is so much time.

MR.

I feel her little hand slide
into mine so easily. She
is up to here, the pocket
of my camel coat, the one
I keep Chiclets in.

Just a little shopping, the
Gimbel's Christmas crowd
around us: a needle in a haystack
if you tried to look for her.

We drift from department to
department; scarves and gloves,
cologne, ladies intimates: how
nice it is to have a little burden
on my arm; why cut this short?

Let's wait till she discovers
who I am, that little face flushed
with embarrassment (or fear?)
How easy it would be to exit onto

Herald Square, Salvation Army
bells, carols, her little voice
impossible to hear above it all.

Here, here, I will say, squeeze
her hand the way her father should
have done before he turned his back.

THE GARDEN OF THE DISPOSSESSED FAVORITES

He fed me apples, young
and yellow, peeled them
with his teeth, told stories
of the war; he was gentle
opening my robe, teasing
my small breasts.

Eunuchs giggled like biddies,
looked for auspicious days.
They hinted that my time
was winding down, someone
else was being groomed, her
tiny hands and feet.

Here is where we must come
when he is done with us, this
garden of deciduous trees
which drop their leaves like
clockwork. Mirrors remind
us how much we have lost.

We plait each other's hair,
make bracelets. The courtiers
giggle; they will bring another
out-of-favor girl who resents
being thrown in with us, a bevvy
of has-beens.

What pleased no longer
pleases. That is the nature
of things: green leaves turn,
papery and brown; a ripe
delicious apple falls, soon
devoured by flies and worms.

Being chosen means we can
never leave; he wants no other
men to have us, lest we
compare. So many days in this
isolated garden, the air reeks
with sounds of aging women.

The scent of frangipani calls
him back, the taste of plums;
I still feel him gently enter from
behind, sing me old lullabies; the
glass bird, the gift he gave me when
I turned twelve.

MUTT

without that dumb dog there would be no warm
against my skin no breathing on the pillow nothing
to feed or clean up crumbs I drop yes I have to take
him out to walk and clean poop those disgusting flies
on top of piles and have the annoying sound of fleas
itching and scratching come to think it's not much
different than morning when my father lifts his
undershirt and scratches in a happy way meaning
he slept good with my baby sister under her Dora
sheets and this dumb dog is better so much better
than a person waking up next to no matter if he
snores he is an old dog who is my warm bed friend
and growls if anyone comes near me most especially
him

REGARDING HISTORY

Nothing interests the slouching boy.
He blanks out while I tutor him;
Wake up, I want to say, someday
history may demand that you enlist,
called to the cradle of man, kill in
places you should have focused on as
we sat hushed among so many books;

you only thought about the soldiers
you would kill this afternoon, *Call of Duty*
on your screen, your mother shouting
from the kitchen that your supper's
getting cold, just like she did last night,
and the night before.

GIVEN

I imagine a soldier's wife hanging the flowered
drapes I gave away; she will sleep next to him,
hope he does not dream. About that boy, no older
than fifteen, ready for heaven; who takes his life,
blows up beside an idling tank. There is no forgetting
the sound, the heat; and what comes afterwards,
retrieving what's left of the kid from some hometown,
just enough to be interred.

That pillowcase his head rests on, the one I never
used; my giveaway will hold the imprint of this man,
patched up, sent home; who might re-up, leaving
his young wife to live alone again; to wait, to iron,
dry laundry on the line; billowing in the late spring
breeze, sheets and pillowcases, Egyptian cotton,
600 count, soft and navy blue.

THIS PLACE, ONCE PARADISE

ONE. A SURFEIT OF WAR

There is always too much. Autumn
leaves are not just oak or sycamore,
but commandoes lowering themselves
to earth. Tree bark is camouflage, olive
and khaki, even the birds follow orders,
what to sing.

We grow drunk on war, toast it in small
cafés: this war's in the desert, the next
at sea; another one, who knows when
or where? Perhaps when we awake, a new
one's being waged. Video pours in; we
watch, hear bombs in the distance.

We will go to the square, alleyways, wide
avenues; comparing notes on the rebels,
gunmen, and their motivations. What
will be gained or lost, who is to blame.
Eventually we will tire of it, monotonous,
omnipresent. All night, all day, all night.

TWO. INTERCEPTS

There is chatter in the air.
They promise something
more spectacular than that
September's toll. From far
away, they murmur their
intentions, keep us guessing.

We go about our ordinary
tasks, dry cleaning, bank
deposits, mail. There is
chatter in the air, plans and
directives, cells poised to
execute at an appointed time.

THREE. WHAT THEY DO NOT KNOW

A man kisses his son good night, the bold
desert moon filling the room with light.
A son's innocent dark hair, sweet pale cheek.
The father's vest is filled with necessary
things, what he needs to take so many lives.
The afterlife awaits, rows of virgins to embrace.

In another house, a daughter
earns a sweet. Her mother takes
her to the candy shop with windows
full of jelly beans and lollipops,
an explosion of colors. A perfect
place to spend a perfect day.

They do not know what will come
this afternoon. The mother wipes
chocolate from her baby's chin, her
sticky hands. Tomorrow they will
visit Grandpa, build castles out of sand,
watch the tide destroy them.

They do not know how sudden it will be,
how quickly it will end. The evening news
will list the lost, speculate about next steps:
a barrage of bombs, soldiers lined thick at the
borders? So many souls took leave from life,
left books and checks and wives.

Estranged husbands; old aunts and little
ones, gone, and a freckled copper-haired girl;
and what becomes of the little boy whose father
lit the fuse? Will he follow suit, identify the
innocent as enemies, long to be delivered to
a string of girls waiting on the other side?

FOUR. LAMENT

There were no fairy tales, just sticks and rocks.
Lullabies my mother sang did not bring you sleep.
You wanted other songs, in another tongue.

My apron was full of fruit. This was paradise once,
the desert rose, persimmon trees, blood oranges and
hibiscus, I wiped juice from the corner of your mouth.

He planted you inside; then left. He left me with
a boy whose hair curled wildly, black as ink, whose
little hand fit mine; so like him, when we were young.

When did you start listening? To voices in the street,
curs howling in the dark, calls to prayer. I did not
raise you, dear boy, to keep company with jackals.

I despise what your father left you; not his charm,
his wit. A restless soul, a lust to avenge sons, their sons,
and the sons of sons: boys like you once were.

You say you must do God's work. What kind of God
would let you board a bus full of the aged, children?
You believe yourself a martyr; I see a sinner, coward.

Forgive me God, my son believed he must answer you.
Take so many innocents. Mothers he left childless,
the children he left motherless. The son you left fatherless.

For now, my grandson walks hand-in-hand with me; I feed
him figs and dates. I watch him pile stones; with one kick,
turns it into rubble. He laughs, begins the game again.

COFFIN SHIP

Fever: the head, the bones, the skin, unbearable;
the journey over months; the evasive shore;
found relics on rocks, children's: perhaps seven
and nine, another, maybe twelve; bones eaten soft
by rickets, the telltale pigeon chest, misshapen spines;
no sun for months, below-board with contagion and
the dead tossed over to the waiting sharks; what must
be done to stave off hunger; from Cobh, Dublin, Galway,
Belfast; to die for a full stomach, bread and fruit and
sunlight through lace curtains and the smell of green.

GRIM REAPER, LIVE AT 11

Another late night show, the bland host, the mediocre band. I've worn my best black robe, brought my polished scythe, but my shoes are scuffed. Pardon me, I've been working overtime and could not get to everything. I understand you've brought a clip, the host says cheerily, and asks for my narration. I am so often a guest, albeit it uninvited, so I oblige. Here's some work I did a while ago, the flood that took so many, some standing on roofs, some paddling furiously, their dogs downstream. And that nursing home which went in one fell swoop!

Now to the desert, so difficult since they're picked off one by one. Wearing so much gear, and the bloody heat—it's a wonder they survive at all. This is my sniper gig, not neat, a contract job. Death sometimes comes with a high price, someone pocketing a chunk of change. I'm ticked about the patched-up boys who really should be gone, their legs AWOL and sometimes their minds. I'm foiled by this crop of docs who mend and mend, so well-trained. And in another place: so many left to bake beneath a crazy country's sun, the men on horseback with their knives and guns and what hangs between their legs: my ambassadors. Then the ordinary stuff, SIDS, AIDS, stage 3 lymphoma: so many ways to stop their clocks.

In closing, I tell the late-night host that the heart's on loan; it's got an expiration date that only I can see. The lights go up, the audience applauds: do they know how soon we'll meet again? Driving home, top down, Jo Stafford's on the radio; did I mention that I love to sing? I do, and she and I are locked in this duet, I'll be Seeing You, that old song, the one that mentions carousels, the small cafes, the wishing well. It ends so beautifully, my eyes well up: yes, I'll be looking at the moon, but I'll be seeing you.

PHOTOGRAPH OVER UKRAINE

You post it before takeoff,
hoping your friends will be
envious. Your first vacation
shot becomes your last.

You will not arrive at the hostel
expecting you by nine; you won't
make the tour of sacred spots,
or eat intriguing foreign food.

The plane is taken down by men
you have no burden with; you are
unaware of borders, grievances,
what fuels their hatred, what

compels them to take the lives
of boys who worked so hard in
school, summer girlfriends, and
teachers who graded their last
exams.

The eerie selfie that you took
is pasted on your Facebook page;
did you for a moment think you'd
have so many likes and comments?

You were invisible as you walked the
high school corridors, scanned
the cafeteria for lunch companions.
It took militants to desecrate your

body, steal the very clothes you wore
to have the pretty girls, who never
knew your name, announce how
much you will be missed, *R.I.P.*

DESCENT

The mountain is peppered
with personal effects. It sounded
like avalanche a villager says,
a jet falling from the sky on
an ordinary Tuesday afternoon.
If one could be grateful, it would
be for this: that it missed houses,
that bodies of students and singers
and writers and baby landed
on the mountain where the snow
took them in like a feather bed.
Let us believe it was thus.

WRECKAGE

Families wait for word.
For floating debris, maybe
a seat or a wrapped gift
which will never reach
its destination.

So far, the ocean gives
up nothing. No black
box, no manifest, not a
body or two, no luggage
with tags and tape.

Another kind of wreckage
stays undersea, at least
that was our intention.
Wedding rings, stolen
goods, snitches, firearms.

Sleeping with the fishes.
Let it be. No search, dredging,
divers. Whatever we tossed
overboard was meant to sink:
no pings, acoustic clues, none.

SOLSTICE

On the long day, when the sun stands still,
how do the evil keep time? Daylight wanes
from here on; are they relieved to have dark
lengthen day by day, a cloak to hide behind?

If they want to make a point, the sun is their
accomplice. More beheadings can be filmed
in natural light, the kidnapped have more time
to see assailants, their countenance.

For those preferring anonymity, dark does
not come soon enough. Light lingers, flouts
bedtime; so the evil take late suppers, wait
for black-night to arrive.

What a relief to have daylight dwindle day
by day; so easy to follow the woman home
from work, get a look at the undressed
girl, pick locks. You can be home by ten.

Such hard work, evil adapting to the light.
But love. It does not have to check its watch;
whether the sun stands still or moves, long
days, long nights, love is constant, impervious.

LEAVE-TAKING

The ways of leave-taking: with sadness,
joyful, reluctant, unexpected. At PDX
I watch departures, a business handshake,
the embrace of relatives and friends, the
perfunctory kiss an antsy child plants on
his grandmother's cheek. But this is none
of these.

She wears a wedding ring and hiking boots,
he is wiry, with the face of someone luck
deserted. They do not seem compatible. He
looks older, not in age but sorrow. She hangs
on to him as if his presence is miraculous,
their bodies cling, there is no other word
for it; ivy and stone, magnet and steel. Are
they lovers, re-united; survivors of the same
avalanche; amicable exes?

It feels like something else, like utter gratitude;
he is the brother she almost lost to heroin, who
stole and spent and lived in gutters, who found
her after years incommunicado, to show her
face to face the answer to her prayers.

UNTIL

She rounds them up and studies how they congregate,
the foreign buzz of them, their lust. My daughter is
entranced, laughs at how they slam against the sides
of bottles she collects them in. How they know the
perfect time to bolt astounds me, as I watch her watching
them, having taken the earth's temperature, these loud
and comely bugs. I tell her how cicadas sleep for years
until the call, how old she'll be when next they'll activate,
how years ago her father lunched with me, our blanket
covered in an eerie tapestry.

I watch her take their wings and test the breeze, and wonder
when she reaches twenty-four if trees will stand, these ones
whose branches host the hordes this June; and am amazed
that these small boys will be men when they arrive again;
and wonder what's become of that young wife who picnicked
full of hope when they last came to ground, a lifetime earlier.

GOOD SON

He goes to Japan to celebrate.
His mother is turning 117;
So many candles on her cake,
on his cake, too, when he turned 92.

In her lifetime, both World Wars,
the remains of cities, and before that,
the Titanic, electric lights; a husband
enthralled by her kimono.

So much to tell great-great-grand-children.
But they are bored with the old lady.
Her body has deflated like a spent
balloon, her mouth like *cho-cho*
fruit, sucked into itself.

This body, once a girl, running with
a kite, so delicate the wind might
kidnap her. When it is time, her son
will hold the string, his mother now
the fragile kite, wait for her to whisper

dear son, you can let go.

www.ingramcontent.com/pod-product-compliance
Lightning Source LLC
La Vergne TN
LVHW051608080426
835510LV00020B/3188